# Lincoln and Douglass

## AN AMERICAN FRIENDSHIP

NIKKI GIOVANNI

ILLUSTRATED BY BRYAN COLLIER

Henry Holt and Company
New York

## AUTHOR'S NOTE

There is a world out there that says the reason people do the right thing is fear: fear of the divine and fear of the pedestrian. I think humans act mostly out of respect. Respect of friendship and respect of the trust that bonds dreams. Lincoln and Douglass had a friendship that helped shape the world. This is just one story about that friendship between those two great men.

## ILLUSTRATOR'S NOTE

In my art for this book, I attempt to show the parallels of Abraham Lincoln's and Frederick Douglass's humble beginnings. I think Douglass's struggle to escape slavery and survive as a free man of color with dignity in the 1800s was much more difficult than Lincoln's youth, but the two men's respective paths to distinction share many elements. Lincoln and Douglass each underwent a challenging journey from illiteracy to an incredible command of language, ideas, profound insight, and persuasive talent. Throughout the book, most action or imagery is behind Lincoln. This composition symbolizes that most of life is behind him—foreshadowing his untimely assassination. Douglass, on the other hand, repeatedly appears with most of the action or imagery to his right, symbolizing that there is still a lot of living to do. In this portrait of a young America, the Civil War rages outside while great orators like Lincoln and Douglass wage political wars to ensure freedom and justice for all. Rooted in these common beliefs, a friendship between Lincoln and Douglass flourished.

Henry Holt and Company, LLC

*Publishers since 1866*

175 Fifth Avenue

New York, New York 10010

www.HenryHoltKids.com

Henry Holt® is a registered trademark of Henry Holt and Company, LLC.

Text copyright © 2008 by Nikki Giovanni

Illustrations copyright © 2008 by Bryan Collier

All rights reserved.

Distributed in Canada by H. B. Fenn and Company Ltd.

Library of Congress Cataloging-in-Publication Data

Giovanni, Nikki.

Lincoln and Douglass : an American friendship / Nikki Giovanni ; illustrated by Bryan Collier.—1st ed.

p.  cm.

ISBN-13: 978-0-8050-8264-7 / ISBN-10: 0-8050-8264-6

1. Lincoln, Abraham, 1809–1865—Juvenile literature.  2. Douglass, Frederick, 1818–1895—Juvenile literature.

3. Presidents—United States—Biography—Juvenile literature.  4. African American abolitionists—Biography—Juvenile literature.

5. Friendship—United States—Juvenile literature.  I. Collier, Bryan, ill.  II. Title.

E457.905.G56 2008    973.7092'2—dc22    [B]    2007050397

First Edition—2008 / Designed by Patrick Collins

Printed in the United States of America on acid-free paper. ∞

1  3  5  7  9  10  8  6  4  2

*Dedicated to all the friends of John Brown*
*—N. G.*


*I dedicate this book to one and all,*
*both young and old, whose efforts for peace and equality*
*continue to be anchored in love for mankind.*
*—B. C.*

By the President of the United States of America:

# A Proclamation

Whereas on the 22nd day of September, A. D. 1862, a proclamation was issued by the President of the United States, containing, among other things, the following, to wit:

"That on the 1st day of January, A. D. 1863, all persons held as slaves within any State or designated part of a State the people whereof shall then be in rebellion against the United States shall be then, thenceforward, and forever free; and the executive government of the United States, including the military and naval authority thereof, will recognize and maintain the freedom of such persons and will do no act or acts to repress such persons, or any of them, in any efforts they may make for their actual freedom.

"That the executive will on the 1st day of January aforesaid, by proclamation, designate the States and parts of States, if any, in which the people thereof, respectively, shall then be in rebellion against the United States; and the fact that any State or the people thereof shall on that day be in good faith represented in the Congress of the United States by members chosen thereto at

elections wherein a major
have participated shall, in
be deemed conclusive evidence
not then in rebellion against

Now, therefore, I, Abr
States, by virtue of the power
the Army and Navy of the U
rebellion against the authority an
as a fit and necessary war measure
this 1st day of January, A. D. 18
so to do, publicly proclaimed for the fu
the first day above mentioned, order an
of States wherein the people thereof, re
against the United States the following,

Arkansas, Texas, Louisiana (except
Palquemines, Jefferson, St. John, St

ty of the qualified voters of such States shall

he absence of strong countervailing testimony,

that such State and the people thereof are

he United States."

ham Lincoln, President of the United

me vested as Commander-In-Chief of

ted States in time of actual armed

government of the United States, and

for suppressing said rebellion, do, on

, and in accordance with my purpose

d period of one hundred days from

d designate as the States and parts

ectively, are this day in rebellion

wit:

he parishes of St. Bernard,

harles, St.

The evening sky was midnight blue. Stars sparkled as brightly as the jewels peeping from the earlobes of the ladies. The hall echoed with the rustle of their dresses, set against the cadence of the gentlemen's boots. The reception for the newly re-elected president of the United States, Abraham Lincoln, was in full swing.

President and Mrs. Lincoln were strolling around the hall arm in arm, greeting friends and supporters. Mrs. Lincoln noticed the president occasionally peering at the door.

"Is something wrong?" she asked.

"I am looking for my friend Frederick Douglass. I had asked him to come and bring his wife."

"Oh, Abraham, not here. Surely you know no Negro should be at the White House."

The president looked at her more with sadness than disappointment. Mrs. Lincoln's sympathies did not lie with the men and women of color seeking to be free. Frederick Douglass, she feared, had persuaded her husband to take up the cause of the enslaved. She did not want to see her beloved South change.

Just then Abraham Lincoln broke into a broad smile. "Here comes my friend Douglass!" he proclaimed as he hurried over to shake hands.

For both men, the journey across the ballroom felt like a journey across time. . . .

*Young Frederick Douglass, refusing to be whipped again, ran away from his owner after fighting with the overseer.*

*He crossed streams and fields until he came to sympathetic Quakers who offered him refuge.*

Young Abraham Lincoln walked five miles back to the country store
because the clerk had given him a nickel too much in change.

*Both young men studied by kerosene light to read the Bible,
print their letters, and better themselves.*

*Douglass worked as a ship's caulker on the Baltimore shore. He longed to sail to freedom on one of the ships that he often watched heading out to sea.*

*The first time Lincoln hauled farm produce down the Mississippi River
to New Orleans, the journey opened his eyes to the world around him.*

When Lincoln was elected to the House of Representatives, Douglass called upon him as he called upon all the newly elected congressmen. Douglass wanted to teach; Lincoln wanted to learn. A friendship flowered based on mutual values, a love of good food, and the ability to laugh even in the worst of times.

**B**oth men hated slavery—Douglass because he had been enslaved; Lincoln because he had seen its evils in New Orleans. Both men knew from their religion and the United States Constitution that human beings should not be "owned" by other human beings. It hurt the goodness and hearts of all. A nation could not exist half enslaved and half free.

Lincoln and Douglass were not the only ones who hated slavery. John Brown hated it, too. A proud, hardworking farmer and white abolitionist, he believed that a man should be able to make a living from the land and take care of his own family. A recent decision to expand slavery into the western territories meant that Brown would have to compete with the larger tracts of land slaveholders commanded. John Brown had not come this far, had not carried his dream of freedom so close to his heart, to let it slip away now. He fought back.

On October 16, 1859, John Brown led several men in an attack on the Harpers Ferry arsenal in Virginia. During the raid, he seized the federal arsenal, killing several people and injuring many more. He intended to arm slaves with weapons from the arsenal and lead them in a war for emancipation.

Abraham Lincoln never met John Brown, but Brown and Frederick Douglass were old friends. The Douglasses were happy to help the abolitionist as much as possible but recognized the attack on Harpers Ferry as a foolhardy mission. They had helped Brown raise funds, though, as did many others, including their good friend Mary Ellen Pleasant. Called Mammy Pleasant by friend and foe alike, she had run away from her Maryland plantation and made her way west, where she began a successful business and became a respected member of the San Francisco community. She, too, hated slavery and went to Virginia to support John Brown's cause.

But the attack on Harpers Ferry failed. Luckily, news of this failure reached Mammy Pleasant before it was too late. She avoided the fate of John Brown and his brave men, who were all hanged.

After the incident at Harpers Ferry, both North and South recognized that war was inevitable. The Republicans had nominated Congressman Abraham Lincoln for president, but the South knew that if Lincoln won, there could be no compromise on the issue of slavery. And, in fact, Lincoln's first four years in office were dominated by the Civil War.

Open
here →

Even on such a grand occasion as the inaugural reception at the White House, the grimness of war hung over the festivities.

Open
←here

"Here you are, Fred," said the president. "I thought I saw you a while ago."

"Yes, sir, you did, but there was a misunderstanding about the door through which I was to enter. The gentlemen invited my wife and me to go around to the rear door, and we declined. No matter. It has been cleared up."

"I'm so sorry," said the president. "I had told my secretary to keep an eye out for you."

Douglass smiled at Lincoln. "I think, sir, you did not mention that we are colored."

"What a long journey, Fred, from the front door to this banister."

"Yes, sir, but not as long as from a plantation in Maryland to freedom. All journeys are long."

"That they are, Fred," said the president. "Yet here we are. We made it. And tonight is a happy night. We must enjoy it. There will be difficult days ahead."

"Yes, sir," agreed Douglass. "But we have the right captain to steer the good ship America. It may not be smooth sailing, but I've no doubt we will make it through."

"With good friends offering wise counsel"—the president smiled—"I don't worry either."

# TIME LINE

**1809** Abraham Lincoln is born on February 12 in a log cabin in Hardin County, Kentucky.

**1816** The Lincolns move to Indiana.

**1818** Frederick Douglass is born as Frederick Augustus Washington Bailey in February in Talbot County, Maryland.

**1827** Douglass learns to read from the daughter of the family that enslaves him. He later learns writing and arithmetic on his own.

**1828** Lincoln takes a flatboat of farm produce to New Orleans, where he witnesses a slave auction.

**1830** The Lincolns move to Illinois.

**1834** Lincoln is elected to the Illinois General Assembly and begins to study law.

**1836** Douglass tries to escape but fails and is sent back to slavery.

**1838** Douglass successfully escapes to New York, then sends for and marries Anna Murray. He changes his name to Frederick Douglass.

**1842** Lincoln marries Mary Todd in Springfield, Illinois.

**1845** Douglass's autobiography, *Narrative of the Life of Frederick Douglass, An American Slave,* is published in May.

**1846** Lincoln is elected to the U.S. House of Representatives.

**1847** Douglass begins printing *The North Star,* an abolitionist newspaper, in December.

**1850** Douglass becomes involved in the Underground Railroad.

**1852** Douglass delivers his famous speech "What to the Slave Is the Fourth of July?" on July 5 in Rochester, New York.

**1860** Lincoln delivers an impassioned antislavery speech on March 6 in New Haven, Connecticut.

Abraham Lincoln is elected the sixteenth president of the United States on November 6.

**1861** Lincoln is inaugurated as president in Washington, D.C. He delivers his first inaugural address on March 4.

The Civil War begins on April 12.

**1863** President Lincoln issues the final Emancipation Proclamation freeing all slaves in Confederate-held territories on January 1.

Lincoln and Douglass meet on August 10; Douglass argues for full equality for African Americans serving in the Union Army. President Lincoln issues Douglass a pass that allows him to cross safely through the Union lines.

**1864** Lincoln and Douglass meet again on August 19, this time to form a plan to rescue blacks from the South in case of a Union defeat.

Abraham Lincoln is re-elected president on November 8.

**1865** Inauguration ceremonies are held in Washington, D.C. President Lincoln delivers his second inaugural address on March 4.

The Civil War ends on April 9.

Lincoln dies after he is shot by John Wilkes Booth on April 14 while attending a play with his wife at Ford's Theater in Washington, D.C. He is buried on May 4 in Oak Ridge Cemetery, outside Springfield, Illinois.

On December 6, Congress ratifies the Thirteenth Amendment to the Constitution abolishing slavery.

**1870** The Fifteenth Amendment granting blacks the right to vote is ratified on February 3.

**1895** Frederick Douglass dies on February 20 in Washington, D.C. He is buried in Mount Hope Cemetery in Rochester, New York.